We Bleed Red

Violet Black

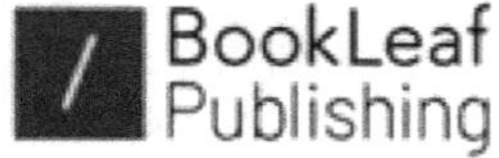

Presentation by *BookLeaf Publishing*

Web: www.bookleafpub.com

E-mail: info@bookleafpub.com

ISBN: 9789357211482

First edition 2022

DEDICATION

Dedicated to my sister and my brothers and my mom and my dad, who inspire me everyday.

Born of Earth and Sky

Child born of sun and moon, dancing upon the
galaxies, with the children of the stars,
constellation eyes, her smile was what caught
my eye, but her mind shone brighter than those
diamond eyes. Star dust sprinkled soul, come fly
with me to the nearest planet, we'll take in all the
sights, and dine on Saturn's rings while we
watch the planets circle 'round their orbits.
Please dance with me upon the moon and I'll
sing to you a tune, and together we'll create our
own axis to which I'll spin you all along.

Child born of seed, blowing across the breeze,
stealing the sun's Rays to shimmer off those
ocean blue eyes, dancing with the daisies,
raising your hands to the sun filled skies, please
carry me away with you to the grass filled
prairies, we can play with the children of the
flowers until we tire, then lay upon the ground
and watch as the grass grows 'round us, oh
flower petal soul, you wish to fly, I dream of
swimming, so take me to the bottom of the sea,
and I'll show you the constellations.

Miss galaxy eyes

Miss galaxy eyes, whispered goodbyes soft kisses on cheeks, do you remember waking from this dream? Yellow music notes and misty eyes remembering the sweetest of songs, never saying I did you wrong, miss galaxy eyes when did things become faulty, when did I forget to call you my darling? Child dies inside my heart far from home in foggy streets missing the punch lines I made for you in the rainy midnight meets, where you would whisper to the moon and make me promise to the stars to love you as long as they burned. I'm sorry I forgot to keep them but please tell me you'll always remember them.

Will you miss my green eyes once they are gone?

Will you please lay my cold body in the warmth of the snow, kiss my black and blue lips goodbye let your salt water tears fall into my open chest, take my melancholy thoughts and fill them with the yellow stars and return them to my open grave, my demons could still wake me from such a deep sleep. Now that I'm a skeleton perhaps I'll fill someone else's closet, will you fall to your knees when mine bend to my own heart? Will you miss my green eyes once they are gone?

Wonderland

Dear hatter you were supposed to come steal me away, dear hatter is wonderland not the place to which sad little girls escape? Red Queen please, I'll do your bidding or you can scream off with my head, but just take me to your castle, I'll paint all your white roses red. Dear Solomon where are your words of wisdom covered in smoke? Dear Solomon why do you hide yourself now that I've grown and can understand your sorrowful tone? Dear hatter, why did you not come steal me away? Because I do understand now why you've all gone mad, it is not living in wonderland at all it, it's living inside your own head. Oh wonderland please, you're the only home for someone as mad as me.

Dear sorrow

Goodbye sweet sorrow, please do come back, but please have mercy on me this time, at least leave a piece of who I was or will be to find after you've gone. Thank you for your visit I do believe I've learned a few things, and I don't blame you sweet sorrow, but I do feel a bit out of place with this new found soul, so please come back, I think I don't quite know who I am when you've gone.

Sierria

Ah what lovely glades she quivers in sounds of sea so far from thee, I do not wish to wake the solem maiden in her dreams, but if she sleeps I lie awake in cold expressions of nights tired grace. Ah but when thou art lonely you needn't anything but think of the shivers the moon doth caress on her face, or her cunning balk as she dances in the wind towards her love who is not thee. Ah if only she would pall me in her sweet embrace how she would quicken me with her grace. But sadly it is not me nor thee but rather the lovely sea which can caress she.

Celestial Ballet

He dances in the skies a celestial ballet at midnight, please can I join you in the starry night. I looked in your eyes and I saw the planets of every galaxy in every corner of the skies, but you said you didn't know why. You smiled at me and I saw the milky ways stars and felt liked I'd touched each one with my own hands but again you said you didn't know why. Can I join your secret dance in the night? Who catches those stargazing eyes? I'm jealous of everyone who does because somehow I know it's not me. So please before we leave, may I have this dance as the stars fall like diamonds around us?

Are You a Dream?

I can only touch you in a dream I can feel your soft lips press to mine, but only when I sleep, I can see your brown eyes and oh how lovely they are in the reflection of a nights fantasy. But darling I do believe you will forever be only a dream, and maybe it makes me crazy to see you so often and waking alone or maybe you're somewhere dreaming of me also.

Pick The Locks

I tear at the white walls, tell me you feel this too,
I claw at the doors, tell me you do too, I punch
at the wood I try to knock through the closed in
room, it's black it wears at my heart it naws on
my soul tell me you know exactly what it does,
or am I the only one who feels it in my bones?

Oh, can you pick the locks, tell me you have the
key or tell me you know the combination to get
in the broken room, with the broken girl. Oh tell
me you can pick the locks.

I remember painting his name on my clean
walls, I remember calling his name into the
darkness, I remember the way it sparked a small
light in it, I remember how it burned my flesh, I
remember wanting to get away but the flames
climb the walls, I kick at the doors.

Oh, can you pick the locks, tell me you have the
key or tell me you know the combination to get
in the broken room, with the broken girl. Oh tell
me you can pick the locks.

It's dark, the fake flames turned to fake ashes,
the room seems bigger in the dim light, it's cold,
the heat vanished and the room seems colder in
the rainy weather.

Oh, can you pick the locks, tell me you have the
key or tell me you know the combination to get
in the broken room, with the broken girl. Oh tell
me you can pick the locks.

Clock (tick, tick, tick)

(Tick, tick, tick) the clock is broken. (Tick, tick, tick)my time is up but my heart keeps beating (tick, tick, tick) my mind is dying but my body's still moving (tick, tick, tick) I want the glass to shatter but the steady rythme keeps beating,(tick, tick, tick) I wish this clock would never have started. (Tick, tick, tick) someone stop the hands please someone shatter the glass. (Tick, tick, tick) the clock is broken. (Tick, tick, tick)

Little Miss Sunshine

Little miss sunshine, tell me did they take your Rain? Little miss sunshine does it hurt to feel no pain? I hope you don't mind if I ask, do you wish to hurt? Little miss sunshine when did the well begin to dry? When did joy and pain begin to evaporate? You look so happy but is it a lie? Darling sunshine, I'm quite sure you used to have a sparkle in your eye, now though I do believe it is very gone , I think perhaps it was replaced with a burning red scar, little miss sunshine, do you dream of feeling something again? Are you quite tired of the callus, or do you prefer the feeling of nothing at all? I'm sorry for the intrusion but please can I ask, do you miss the feel of water on your face? Little miss sunshine tell me, would you prefer to drown, or are you perfectly fine to suffocate?

Black Roses

Black caskets laid in my corpse, cold gravestones of open scars, will you lay down in the roses of my soul or let yourself fall between the solidified masses of my lost dreams if all I could do was slowly weep, will you say goodnight to the sweet child with open wounds of forgotten memories, or will you force her to grow up into a remembered symphony? I'll say goodbye but never forever, the cold and embittered stars will whisper of our song evermore.

Bottled Emotions and Watered Roses

There's an empty space in my hand, between my cold fingers, that only you could fill, please wrap you warm body around my forbidden and icy soul, perhaps it would melt into yours. I hide knives inside my coats, armor under all my clothes so I never have to feel the arrows shot at my heart and soul, august snow and January rain, nothing seems to connect inside of my brain. Bottled emotions and watered roses growing inside my home, good intentions but missed expressions and never letting things just be existing. we're all just pretending to remember and trying our best to keep it together.

Hello, goodbye.

You know how in all the fairy tales and movies and books they never know what they have so they leave or they wait but they always come back like waves crashing to the shore? I don't know, I just wish I believed in fairy tales because I'm so afraid you'll never crash into me and I've already fallen so deep into your black waters

If I Jump Will You Follow?

Too afraid to jump but somehow I dance on the edge with you unafraid to slip. Did you take my hand or did I take yours? All I remember is it was something warm in all the darkness. You held me close and laughed, something about not knowing how to dance, but all I felt was your heartbeat on my hands. Your arms felt like home but that scared me too much to hold on and I let go. Can you forgive me for letting go?

Wild Night Air

Ah, how I do miss the smell of the wild night air, please take me back, I belong to the moon I do not belong to you, I miss my friends of the forest, I miss seeing them dance in the wild night air, I left in search of me, but I believe I lost her somewhere blowing in the midnight breeze, I traversed the skies I sailed the oceans, now all I really want is to go breath in the wild night air, I think this life is just a little to complicated, and I think this world is just a little to quick for me, I think the Earth needs, just for a moment, to stop spinning, ah how I do wish to go slow, how I do love the leisurely pace of the moon, I wish to go on a midnight walk, you could come along, but let us not talk, for fear our voices might disturb the wild night air.

Stardust

And one night she watched in wonder when the bright turned to dark as the stars fell from heaven, into the ocean they sank, entangled in the seaweed they became, as she swam to the bottom where they lay, she stared in wonder as they broke into pieces and sprinkled star dust in the water and air, it wrapped around her and flowed into her veins, it sank itself into the bottom of her heart and inside her soul it sang, she danced alone in her room with it's tune and it's arms wrapped about her, everyone said she was a dreamer and a little out of place, but it was as it should be, for she was made of star dust amongst people made only of flesh.

My heart

Settle down my love we're perfectly fine. Settle
down my darling it's all just new.
Wake from your dream it will be okay, just don't
say goodbye to all of them because you think it's
too late.
Settle down my heart I'll never leave you on
your own.
Settle down sweet child I'll love you forever.
I know you don't believe it but the world is here
for you to discover, I wish I could make you see
it but the stars hardly shine as bright as you.
Settle down sweet child the world is here for
Our taking.

www.ingramcontent.com/pod-product-compliance
Lightning Source LLC
La Vergne TN
LVHW050311200726
843509LV00015B/3280